STU

STUDY GUIDE

COMPANION TO CD/DVD MESSAGE SERIES

the
BLESSED
Life

UNLOCKING THE REWARDS
OF GENEROUS LIVING

ROBERT MORRIS

**GATEWAY®
PRESS**

The Blessed Life Study Guide
Copyright © 2016 Gateway Publishing®

ISBN: 978-1-949399-92-9
eBook ISBN: 978-1-949399-93-6

19 20 21 22   6 5 4

www.gatewaypublishing.com
www.theblessedlife.gatewaypeople.com

CONTENTS

IT'S ALL ABOUT
THE HEART

The Lord cares most about our hearts. God does not simply bless our giving; He blesses giving from the right attitude of our hearts. As we develop grateful hearts, we remove selfishness and giving becomes joyful.

ENGAGE

What is the most selfless thing you've ever seen someone do?

-Or-

What is the most unselfish thing another person has ever done for you?

WATCH

Watch Robert Morris in "It's All About the Heart." As you view it:

- Listen to God's perspective on giving — not just giving money, but having a generous heart.
- Watch for the key to working selfishness and greed out of your heart.

(If you are not able to watch this teaching on video, read the following. Otherwise, skip to the **Talk** section after viewing.)

READ

The Lord cares most about our hearts. God does not bless our giving; He blesses giving from the right attitude of our hearts. When we give, we receive blessings; however, that should not be our main motivation for giving. We must confront any selfishness in our hearts.

Jesus says,

> "Judge not, and you shall not be judged. Condemn not, and you shall not be condemned. Forgive, and you will be forgiven. Give, and it will be given to you: good measure, pressed down, shaken together, and running over will be put into your bosom. For with the same measure that you use, it will be measured back to you" (Luke 6:37–38).

Often people hear teaching or think these verses are about money. In fact, they do not speak about money at all. This passage does address giving, but Jesus' teaching here actually applies to every area of our lives because of the laws of sowing and reaping. If you plant or give a seed, you don't just get back one seed in return. You get back a tree or a plant that has produced many seeds. And that's the way God works; whatever you give, you're going to get more back.

Consequently, we benefit much more by giving good things rather than bad things, because we are going to get more of what-ever we have given. This truth becomes clear when we consider the larger context of these verses. For example, back up one more verse and look at what Jesus says in context:

> "Therefore be merciful, just as your Father also is merciful. Judge not, and you shall not be judged. Condemn not, and you shall not be condemned. Forgive, and you will be forgiven" (Luke 6:36-37).

Only then does Jesus say, "Give and it will be given to you" (Luke 6:38). Yes, this principle does apply to money, but a person can also give forgiveness. We can give mercy. We can give understanding, patience, time, or service. Jesus simply speaks about the broad principle of giving. Whatever you give will also be given back to you in "good measure, pressed down, shaken together, and running over." You get back so much more than you actually give. If you give judgment to someone, you will get judgment in return. However, it will be "pressed down, shaken together, and running over." Consider carefully what you are giving.

The basic problem with most teaching about giving based upon Luke 6:38 is that teachers present material gain as the primary motive for giving. God doesn't want us to catch the vision of getting; He wants us to catch the vision of giving.

In order to become generous givers, we must first confront the problem of a selfish heart. God cares very much about our hearts. Deuteronomy 15:7-15 directly addresses these matters of the heart in terms of generosity and giving. In this passage, Moses exhorts God's people to give generously and willingly to those who need help. Moses says, "You shall surely give to him, and your heart should not be grieved when you give to him, because for this thing the Lord your God will bless you in all your works and in all to which you put your hand" (Deuteronomy 15:10). If a person refused to give to a fellow Israelite by thinking that the debt wouldn't be repaid before the Year of Jubilee (the year when all debts were cancelled or forgiven), then this refusal would be a direct violation of God's command. God does not want us to have selfish, begrudging hearts. God wants us to be generous because He is generous.

God did not create generosity because He needs our money or resources. God owns everything, and if He did need something, he could create more of it. The reason God created giving was for our benefit. Giving, more than any other activity that we as believers can do, works selfishness and greed out of our hearts and lives.

In addition to dealing with our selfish hearts, God wants us to take care our grieving hearts. In the Bible passage we just read from Deuteronomy, God specifically says, "You shall not be grieved when you give to Him." Selfishness attacks us before we give, and grief attacks us after we give. Often the reason a person grieves after giving is because of a false perspective that he is the owner, and not the steward, of his possessions. However, God is the owner because everything belongs to Him. In our short lives, we have the opportunity to steward various resources that come our way, but God already owns all of it.

If the teller at the bank handed you one hundred dollars from money already in your account, the bank would not grieve over giving it to you, because it already belongs to you. In the same way, when we give to God, we can do so without grieving if we realize that He already owns it. The fact is this: God doesn't bless giving. He blesses giving from the right attitude of our heart.

God said He wants us not only to give, but also to be generous. The first time we are born in the natural, we are born selfish. Every parent knows children have to be taught how to share because they don't do it naturally. But when we are born again, we are born generous. God wants us to be generous just as He is generous.

At the end of the Scripture passage in Deuteronomy 15, Moses says, "From what the Lord your God has blessed you with, you shall give to Him. You shall remember that you were a slave in the land of Egypt, and the Lord your God redeemed you; therefore I command you this thing today" (Deuteronomy 15:14–15). Why did God instruct the Israelites to remember that they had been slaves? Because it would fill their hearts with gratitude for what He had done for them.

When we allow God to remind us that we used to be slaves to sin and that everything we have is by His gracious hand, this knowledge will help us to be grateful. And when we're grateful, it's easy to be generous. Genuine gratitude to God is a rare and powerful thing. And a heart of gratitude is a vital key to cultivating a lifestyle of generosity. When other people ask Debbie, "Why do you think Robert is so generous?" Her answer is simple, "Because he's never gotten over getting saved. He's never forgotten where he came from. And he knows that everything we have came from the Lord." Always remember what God has done for you. It will make generosity a natural response from your heart.

NOTES

_____

_____

_____

_____

_____

TALK

For group discussion or personal reflection:

QUESTION 1

In the past, what teaching did you hear about giving? Did these teachings have a positive or negative effect on you? Explain.

_____

_____

_____

_____

QUESTION 2

Read Luke 6:37-38:

> Judge not, and you shall not be judged. Condemn not, and you shall not be condemned. Forgive, and you will be forgiven. Give, and it will be given to you: good measure, pressed down, shaken together, and running over will be put into your bosom. For with the same measure that you use, it will be measured back to you.

People often equate this passage with money, yet money is not mentioned. Some have called this the "Spiritual Law of Reciprocity" — whatever you give (judgment, mercy, time, service) will be returned to you in abundance. What are some areas of your life where you've seen this "sowing and reaping" principle at work in the past — for either good or bad?

_____

_____

_____

_____

_____

QUESTION 3

Why do you think people sometimes struggle with selfishness before giving and grief after they have given?

_____

_____

_____

_____

Follow-up Question

Can you think of a time you've struggled with either selfishness or grief when giving?

_____

_____

_____

_____

Follow-up Question

What are some practical ways you can work through those initial struggles in your heart and choose to have generosity with a grateful heart?

_____

_____

_____

_____

QUESTION 4

"Giving to get" seems to have become the standard approach many have taken to motivate believers to share. In what ways does the declaration "God doesn't bless giving; He blesses giving with the right heart" challenge what you have been taught in the past about giving?

_____

_____

_____

_____

WHERE IS MY MONEY GOING?	
My top five categories of discretionary spending (e.g., eating out, entertainment, ministry giving, travel, recreation, etc.):	
Category	**Average Monthly Spending**

QUESTION 5

People can give of their treasure, time, and talents. How does the way people spend their time, give of their treasure, and use their talents show where their heart is? In which of these areas are you the most generous? Which is the greatest challenge?

_____

_____

_____

_____

_____

PRAY

Take some time as a group to pray for each other as you think about the truths discussed in this session.

EXPLORE

Do you want to go deeper with this teaching? Here are some additional things to think about, pray for, or write about in your journal throughout the next week:

KEY QUOTE

Giving, more than any other activity that a believer does, works selfishness and greed out of our lives.

—Robert Morris

One hindrance to having a generous heart is believing that what you have is yours instead of God's. How does having a proper perspective about God being the owner of everything make it easier for you to give? What are some practical ways for you to be aware of your status as a steward rather than the owner?

When you have a grateful heart for all God has done for you and remember all He has given you, giving back to Him is easy. List some of the things God has done for you and given to you:

_____

_____

_____

_____

_____

KEY VERSES

Deuteronomy 15:7–15, Malachi 3:8–12, Matthew 6:21, Luke 6:37–38

What truths stand out to you as you read these verses?

_____

_____

_____

_____

_____

What is the Holy Spirit saying to you through these Scriptures?

_____

_____

_____

_____

_____

KEY QUESTION

If your heart tends to gravitate toward those things you have invested in most heavily, what does your discretionary spending say about your passions and priorities? What about those things on which you have not spent money? Where would you like for your heart to be?

KEY PRAYER

Father, help me cultivate a grateful heart toward You. Remind me of all You have done for me and all You have delivered me from. Produce in me a lifestyle of generosity and the grace of giving. In Jesus' name, Amen.

02

WHAT TEST?

Tithing — offering to God the first tenth of our increase or income —
is a biblical concept originating before the Law and continuing through
the New Testament. Tithing is a test of our love for, trust in, and obedience
to our Heavenly Father.

RECAP

In the previous segment, we were encouraged to examine ourselves for traces of a selfish or "grieving" heart where material things are concerned. We were also reminded to meditate on all God has done for us in order to cultivate in us a heart of gratitude. We learned that a generous heart is the key to dealing with selfishness in our lives.

Describe any moments this week in which these issues came to mind. Has God given you an opportunity to act in generosity? If so, how did you respond?

ENGAGE

You may have experienced a nightmare that many people report. You go back to school as a younger person, only to discover to your horror

---

that the teacher has handed out an important exam. In the dream, you arrive very late and unprepared! Why do you think so many people report this nightmare? Do you have any stressful or humorous recurring dreams?

WATCH

Watch Robert Morris in "What Test?" As you view it:

- Look for the symbolic significance of the number "10" in Scripture.
- Listen for the principle of tithing before the Law and in the New Testament.

(If you are not able to watch this teaching on video, read the following. Otherwise, skip to the **Talk** section after viewing.)

READ

When you were in school, did you ever arrive at a class only to find that the rest of the students were pulling out pencils, preparing to take a test you had forgotten about? After you realized the teacher was giving a test, were the first words out of your mouth: "What Test?" Many people don't realize this, but tithing represents a test for every believer.

The word translated "tithe" in the Bible actually means "tenth" or "a tenth part." Many people don't know that the number ten, as used in the Bible, has rich symbolic significance. Just as recurring numbers such as seven and forty carry special meaning, the same is true with the number ten.

The authors of the Bible consistently associated the number ten with "testing." For example, in the book of Exodus, God tested Pharaoh's heart with ten plagues or signs. God delivered His standard of righteousness, which tests our conduct, in the form of Ten Commandments. The children of Israel experienced ten specific tests or trials while wandering in the wilderness. In the book of Genesis, young Jacob worked for his future father-in-law Laban. During that season, God tested Jacob's loyalty and character ten times in the form of unjust changes in his wages. And the first chapter of the book of Daniel, he is tested for ten days. This pattern continues into the New Testament. In Matthew 25, ten virgins are tested for their preparedness. Revelation 2:10 mentions ten days of testing.

With this biblical pattern for the number ten, we shouldn't be surprised to learn that tithing or giving one-tenth of our increase back to God, tithing, represents a key test for us as God's children. But it also represents a test for God! The prophet Malachi said that the Lord declares:

"Bring all the tithes into the storehouse,
That there may be food in My house,
And try Me now in this,"
Says the LORD *of hosts,*
"If I will not open for you the windows of heaven
And pour out for you such blessing
That there will not be room enough to receive it." (Malachi 3:10,
    emphasis added).

This passage about tithing is the only place in the Bible where we are encouraged to "test" God. At the same time, the tithe represents the ultimate test for the heart of the believer.

The Bible delivers a clear message about tithing. Moses said, "All the tithe of the land, whether of the seed of the land or of the fruit of the tree, is the Lord's. It is holy to the Lord" (Leviticus 27:30).

However, today some believers argue against tithing because they say it is a part of the Old Covenant Law, which God replaced with the New Covenant. Yes, tithing was a part of the Law. However, the Bible shows that the principle of the tithe existed hundreds of years before the Law even existed. It is a principle of God, not simply an Old Covenant Law. In Genesis 14, Abraham paid a tithe (one tenth) of everything he gained in battle to Melchizedek (an Old Testament type of Christ). In Genesis 28, Jacob told God he would give Him a tenth of all his increase. The Patriarchs (early fathers of Israel) understood and honored the principle of tithing long before the Law was written. In the next session, we will look at an example that happened hundreds of years even before these instances.

Not only is tithing a clear biblical principle that existed long before the Law, but the New Testament also mentions it. Jesus himself, when talking to the Pharisees in Luke 11, told them that although they tithed on their herbs, they neglected the weightier matters of the Law. Jesus continues by saying: "These you ought to have done, without leaving the others undone" (Luke 11:42). Jesus told them that they should both tithe as well as address the

weightier matters of the Law. If Jesus says we should tithe . . .
we should tithe.

Malachi quoted another strong statement from the Lord:

> *"Will a man rob God?*
> *Yet you have robbed Me!*
> *But you say,*
> *'In what way have we robbed You?'*
> *In tithes and offerings.*
> *You are cursed with a curse,*
> *For you have robbed Me,*
> *Even this whole nation" (Malachi 3:8–9).*

God not only says that we can rob Him when we don't give tithes and offerings, but He also says we are cursed with a curse. This matter is obviously serious to the Lord. Yet some believers resist this teaching and argue that New Testament believers cannot possibly experience a curse in their finances because Jesus bore the curse of sin for us all on the cross. There is indeed a wonderful spiritual truth in Paul's words to the Galatians:

> Christ has redeemed us from the curse of the law, having become a curse for us (for it is written, *"Cursed is everyone who hangs on a tree"*), that the blessing of Abraham might come upon the Gentiles in Christ Jesus, that we might receive the promise of the Spirit through faith (Galatians 3:13–14).

Certainly, Jesus bore more than we can possibly imagine on the cross. Yet, it is still possible to experience the effects of the curse, even though Christ took those effects fully upon Himself. We must all appropriate or take possession of by faith what Jesus did for us on the cross. And when we do not, we continue to experience some of the effects of the curse.

If we disobey God's Word as believers, we can and do experience the negative consequences of sin. This truth applies to our finances just as surely as it applies to anything else in our lives. Can we, if we are in willful violation of God's principles of firstfruits and the tithe, see our finances come under a curse? Yes, we can.

The Ten Commandments are the foundation of the Old Covenant Law. If you break one of those Old Covenant commands and murder someone, you would still experience consequences. If you commit adultery, there will be consequences. Even though Jesus redeemed us from the curse of the Law, we still see that consequences remain for living against God's principles.

God gave the command that all His people are to tithe; however, with our obedience also comes a blessing. The believer's tithe helps support the work of the church, the priest, and the ministry to people. The place where we receive our "spiritual food" is the place where we are to pay our tithes. You would never go to a restaurant and eat a meal, and then leave without paying the bill. Yet people who don't tithe come to the church and eat a "spiritual" meal, and leave without paying the bill, so to speak. Practically speaking, it is the tithe that allows pastors and ministers to spend their time preparing spiritual meals and feeding the people.

In the Bible, the church is referred to as the bride of Christ. What if Jesus gave you one thousand dollars a week, but asked you to give ten percent to His bride while he was away. Would you do it? How would Jesus see the person who gave what He asked to His bride? What about the person who gave extra? What about the person who gave less, or not at all? Tithing is personal to Jesus because it is for His bride.

Obeying God's Word through tithing breaks the curse and invites God's blessings and provision for our lives and finances. It is a test. Will you pass the test?

_____

_____

_____

_____

TALK
For group discussion or personal reflection:

QUESTION 1
Many believers struggle when it comes to tithing. Why do you think this happens? What are some of the barriers or misunderstandings that hinder believers from tithing?

_____

_____

_____

_____

QUESTION 2

Through disobedience to God's principles, it is possible to step out from under God's protective umbrella of favor and protection. Perhaps you have experienced that in some area of your life other than finances. If you are comfortable talking about it, what were the consequences and what did you do to realign your life with God's Word and will?

_____

_____

_____

_____

QUESTION 3

Have you tended to view tithing as a burden or a benefit? What practical steps could you take to keep the benefits of tithing in mind?

_____

_____

_____

_____

QUESTION 4

The author of Hebrews suggests that when we tithe here on earth, Jesus spiritually receives those tithes in heaven (Hebrews 7:8). How does that knowledge influence the attitude of your heart as you bring your tithes and offerings to God?

_____

_____

_____

_____

QUESTION 5

Read Deuteronomy 26:1-2 and Deuteronomy 26:13-15.

And it shall be, when you come into the land which the LORD your God is giving you *as* an inheritance, and you possess it and dwell in it, that you shall take some of the first of all the produce of the ground, which you shall bring from your land that the LORD your God is giving you, and put *it* in a basket and go to the place where the LORD your God chooses to make His name abide (Deuteronomy 26:1-2).

Then you shall say before the LORD your God: "I have removed the holy *tithe* from *my* house, and also have given them to the Levite, the stranger, the fatherless, and the widow, according to all Your commandments which You have commanded me; I have not transgressed Your commandments, nor have I forgotten *them*. I have not eaten any of it when in mourning, nor have I removed *any* of it for an unclean *use,* nor given *any* of it for the dead. I have obeyed the voice of the LORD my God, and have done according to all that You have commanded me. Look down from Your holy habitation, from heaven, and bless Your people Israel and the land which You have given us, just as You swore to our fathers, 'a land flowing with milk and honey'" (Deuteronomy 26:13–15).

According to these Bible passages, what is the tithe, and to whom or what are we to give it?

_____

_____

_____

_____

PRAY

Take some time as a group to pray for each other in the light of the truths discussed in this session.

EXPLORE

Do you want to go deeper with this teaching? Here are some additional things to think about, pray for, or write about in your journal throughout the next week:

KEY QUOTE

The tithe is personal to Jesus. It helps take care of His bride.

—*Robert Morris*

Are you currently tithing? If not, what are the reasons? How can you overcome the things in your heart that keep you from tithing? Ask the Holy Spirit to help you and make a plan to begin tithing.

_____

_____

_____

_____

KEY VERSES

Malachi 3: 8–12, Deuteronomy 15:20, Matthew 5:17–20, Matthew 23:23, Hebrews 7:8, 1 John 3:18-22

What stands out to you as you read these Bible passages?

_____

_____

_____

_____

_____

What is the Holy Spirit saying to you through these Scriptures?

_____

_____

_____

_____

_____

KEY QUESTION

Considering your understanding of God's Word and given that tithing is a test, what are the benefits of passing this test?

_____

_____

_____

_____

_____

KEY PRAYER

Father, give me the courage, trust, and faith in Your goodness to bring the whole tithe into Your storehouse. Give me the fuller revelation that when I tithe, Jesus Himself receives it. And put in me a sensitive, generous heart that promptly responds when Your Holy Spirit nudges me to give and share from the resources you have put in my trust. In Jesus' name, Amen.

03

THE PRINCIPLE OF FIRST

The principle of first is about making sure God is first in our lives. In Exodus, God told Moses to consecrate the firstborn among the children and the animals. Throughout Scripture, the firstborn always belonged to the Lord. Our obedience to God's principles reveals the condition of our hearts.

RECAP

In the previous section, we discussed tithing as a test. We learned how God tests our hearts when we make a decision whether to tithe. When we tithe we are redeemed from the curse and God blesses us. Can you see a difference when you live according to God's Word and when you don't? How did last week's session challenge you or cause you to think?

ENGAGE

"Firsts" are always memorable: Your first trip overseas; your first paying job; or the first baby you bring home from the hospital. Share a brief story about one of these "firsts" in your life and tell why it was so special or interesting.

WATCH

Watch Robert Morris in "The Principle of First." As you view it:

- Consider how faith is required to offer a firstfruits offering.
- Look for the place God has in all creation, and how your actions put God first in your own life.

(If you are not able to watch this teaching on video, read the following. Otherwise, skip to the **Talk** section after viewing.)

READ

The principle of first emerges throughout the Bible, both in the Old and New Testaments. When we give the first to God, we put God first in our life. Exodus 13:2 very clearly illustrates this principle. In this passage, God says, "Consecrate to Me all the firstborn, whatever opens the womb among the children of Israel, both of man and beast; it is Mine." God plainly declares that the firstborn is "Mine." It belongs to Him. In fact, sixteen times in Scripture, God declares that the first-born is His! For example, Exodus 13:12, 13 says:

> That you shall set apart to the LORD all that open the womb, that is, every firstborn that comes from an animal which you have; the males shall be the LORD's. But every firstborn of every donkey you shall redeem with a lamb; and if you will not redeem it, then you shall break its neck. And all the firstborn of man among your sons you shall redeem (NKJV).

According to Old Testament Law, the firstborn was to be either sacrificed or redeemed. This principle is critical. No third option existed. Every time the Israelites' livestock animals delivered their firstborn, they were to sacrifice it. If it was designated an unclean animal (a donkey, for example), the Israelites had to redeem it with a clean, spotless lamb. To summarize, the Israelites had to sacrifice the clean firstborn, and the unclean firstborn had to be redeemed.

With that principle in mind, think about the account of John the Baptist meeting Jesus on the banks of the Jordan River. One day, John was baptizing people, and he looked up to see Jesus walking toward him. At that point, John cried out, "Behold! The Lamb of God who takes away the sin of the world!" (John 1:29).

With that inspired declaration, John perfectly defined the role Jesus had come to fulfill. Jesus was God's firstborn. Jesus was clean—perfect and unblemished in every way. On the other hand, every other human was born unclean. We were all born sinners with a fully active sin nature. If you're a parent, think about your children. You don't have to teach them to do wrong things—they naturally do wrong things. Instead, you have to teach them how to be good. All of us were born unclean, and with a sin nature.

Now think back to the principle of the firstborn in Exodus. The Law stated that if the firstborn animal were clean, the Israelites should sacrifice it. But if the firstborn were unclean, they should redeem it with a clean animal. Do you see the symbolic parallel? Jesus Christ was God's spotless Lamb. But every one of us was born unclean; therefore, Jesus was sacrificed to redeem us.

When Jesus redeemed us by His sacrifice, He bought us back for God. Jesus was actually a firstfruits offering. In reality, Jesus was

God's tithe. Is it any wonder that the tithe is such a serious and holy thing to God? God gave His tithe — Jesus — in faith before we ever believed. Romans 5:8 says, "But God demonstrates His own love toward us, in that while we were still sinners, Christ died for us" (NKJV).

We have to give our firstfruits offering—our tithe—in much the same way. Before we see the blessing of God, we must give it in faith. Before we know if we're going to have any "month left over at the end of our money," we give in faith and trust. It is not the act of giving ten percent that God blesses—God blesses our faith. It takes faith to give the firstfruits. It doesn't take faith to give the leftovers. When a firstborn lamb is birthed into a flock, it is not possible to know how many more lambs that ewe will produce. God didn't instruct the Israelites to take one out of every ten lambs born, but rather, to give the first lamb. It is an act of faith.

It always requires faith to give the first to God. That's why so few Christians experience the blessings of tithing. It requires giving to God before you see if you're going to have enough. By tithing, it is as if we are saying to God, "I recognize You first. I am putting You first in my life, and I trust You to take care of the rest of the things in my life." As with most matters in the Christian life, it comes down to the attitude of our hearts. The question is, "Do I trust God enough to give the first part to Him?"

We give God our firstfruits because God is first in creation. In fact, God cannot be second. When you study the attributes of God, you will realize that God is omniscient. He knows everything and cannot have thoughts like we have. We think to figure things out. God never figures anything out, because He already knows the answer. In the same way, God is immutable: He cannot change. If God could change, He could improve. God cannot improve because He is already perfect. When you study the attributes of God, you will discover that God cannot be second. God can only be first.

In Genesis 4:3-4, God honored Abel's offering but not Cain's. The reason is because Abel's offering was from the firstborn of his flock; however, Cain's offering was not from his firstfruits. The Bible says, "*In the process of time, it came to pass* that Cain brought *an offering* of the fruit of the ground to the Lord. Abel also brought of the *firstborn* of his flock and of their fat. And the Lord respected Abel and his offering, but He did not respect Cain and his offering" (NKJV, emphasis added). God could not respect Cain's offering because it was not his first. God can only be first, He cannot accept second.

Proverbs 3:9-10 says that we are to honor the Lord with our possessions and with the firstfruits of all our increase. When we honor Him in this way, we invite God's blessing into our lives, and "your barns will be filled with plenty, and your vats will overflow." Many blessings go along with tithing, but it is the principle of faith and putting God first that initiates these blessings. The first portion, the tithe, is the portion that redeems the rest. God does not desire a legalistic, begrudging response. He desires for us to submit our hearts to Him in joy and in the faith that His principles are true.

When you put God first in your life and honor Him with your tithe, it is a witness to your family. There is a powerful verse in Exodus 13:8 which says, "And you shall tell your son in that day, saying, '*This is done* because of what the LORD did for me when I came up from Egypt'" (NKJV). When your children see you honor God, and they ask you why you tithe, you have the opportunity to tell them how you were a slave, lost and dead in sin; and then Jesus, God's tithe, came and redeemed you. With a grateful heart, you can explain: "This is why I put God first in my life."

TALK

For group discussion or personal reflection:

QUESTION 1

What are some of the attributes of God that make you feel the most reverent or in awe of who He is? Does it make it easier or harder for you to honor God with your firstfruits when you take time to think about His attributes?

_____

_____

_____

_____

_____

QUESTION 2

What types of fears or concerns do you wrestle with most when thinking about the principle of first? Why is it sometimes easier to believe we are saved by faith than it is to believe, by faith, that God will bless us and take care of our needs?

_____

_____

_____

_____

QUESTION 3

God accepted Abel's offering, but not Cain's because Abel gave his as a firstfruits offering, and Cain did not. If you have started tithing by faith, how does this principle affect when and how you tithe? In what way does the timing stretch your faith?

_____

_____

_____

_____

_____

QUESTION 4

"There is one who scatters, yet increases more; and there is one who withholds more than is right, but it leads to poverty" (Proverbs 11:24). God makes sure that any first thing given to Him is never lost. But as this verse in Proverbs reminds us, what we unjustly withhold from God, we will lose. In what ways have you seen this principle at work in your life or in the life of someone close to you?

_____

_____

_____

_____

QUESTION 5

Every time we are paid, an inescapable moment of "worship" imme-diately follows. The first place to which we direct a portion of that money reveals something about what is "first" in our lives. What kinds of financial things are most likely to compete for "first place" in your heart?

_____

_____

_____

_____

PRAY

Take some time as a group to pray for each other in light of the truths discussed in this session.

EXPLORE

Do you want to go deeper with this teaching? Here are some additional things to think about, pray for, or write about in your journal throughout the next week:

KEY QUOTE

It takes faith to give the first portion to God.

—Robert Morris

We all have areas in which we find it easier to trust the Lord, while in other areas we seem to struggle to rest in His promises. Respond to the following:

I find it easy to trust God about:

_____

_____

_____

_____

_____

_____

Sometimes I struggle to trust God concerning:

_____

_____

_____

_____

_____

KEY VERSES

Exodus 13:1, Matthew 16:25, Exodus 2:11–16, Proverbs 3:9, 10,
Romans 11:16, 1 Corinthians 15:20-23, 1 Corinthians 16:1, 2

What stands out to you as you read these verses?

_____

_____

_____

_____

_____

What is the Holy Spirit saying to you through these Scriptures?

_____

_____

_____

_____

_____

KEY QUESTION

If you were to give the firstfruits of your talents, what would that look like? In what ways can you honor God at the beginning of everything you do? How can you remind yourself to do this on a regular basis?

_____

_____

_____

_____

_____

KEY PRAYER

Heavenly Father, thank You for teaching us Your ways and the principle of first. Give us greater revelation and understanding about Your heart and the purpose for tithing. Please help us to have faith to give You the first of all our increase. Help us to fully submit our hearts to You in all our ways. In Jesus' name, Amen.

04

BREAKING THE
SPIRIT OF MAMMON

Mammon originates from a word meaning "riches," and it is actually a spirit. Jesus said, "You cannot serve God and mammon" (Matthew 6:24). Our money can either be submitted to God or a spirit of mammon.

RECAP

In the previous section, we discussed the eternal, spiritual principle of firstfruits. During the past week, did you encounter any opportunities to show God that He is first in your life? Did your actions test your level of trust in His faithfulness and goodness?

ENGAGE

One recent study showed that 70% of lottery winners squander their wealth within a few years. And a recent documentary explored the fact that many people who win the lottery find that sudden, unearned wealth utterly ruins their lives. Why do you think this is the case?

WATCH

Watch Robert Morris in "Breaking the Spirit of Mammon." As you view it:

- Look for the link between the spirit of mammon and the Antichrist.
- Listen for the key to breaking a spirit of mammon.

(If you are not able to watch this teaching on video, read the following. Otherwise, skip to the **Talk** section after viewing.)

READ

The word *mammon* only occurs four times in the New Testament in Jesus' teaching. Luke 16:9–16 contains three of these occurrences. The fourth is in a parallel passage in Matthew 6. Jesus used the word *mammon* as a name here to indicate that He was talking about some kind of demonic spirit or false god.

Mammon comes from an Aramaic word that means "riches." Mammon does not mean money, rather mammon is actually a spirit. The Assyrians (one of the people groups who speak Aramaic) borrowed the concept of a "god of wealth" from their Babylonian neighbors. Babylon was a city founded on pride and arrogance. The history of their pride goes all the way back to the account of the tower of Babel in Genesis 11. At its heart, pride is an attitude that says, "We don't need God. We're self-sufficient." This is what the spirit of mammon tries to tell us as well: "You don't need God. Trust in riches!" The word *Babylon* essentially means: "sown in confusion." Mammon, with its roots in Babylonian history, still brings confusion to this day. Mammon is the spirit of the world and the spirit that rests on money not submitted to God.

Jesus makes a very strong statement about the spirit of mammon. He says emphatically, "You cannot serve God and mammon" (Matthew 6:24). The spirit of mammon diametrically opposes God. You cannot follow the god of this world, while at the same time, follow the One True God. It is impossible to serve both at the same time. Jesus says that you will love one and hate the other. You will be loyal to one and despise the other.

Mammon tries to take the place of God. Mammon promises us those things that only God can give—security, significance, identity, independence, power, and freedom. Mammon tells us that it can insulate us from life's problems and that money is the answer to every situation. Mammon wants to rule your life, and is attempting to steal your heart away from trusting in God.

The reason we cannot serve God and mammon is that the spirit of mammon is the opposite of the Spirit of God. Mammon tells us to take and hoard; God says to give and trust. Mammon is selfish; God is generous. Mammon is nothing more than the system of this fallen world that stands in sharp opposition to God and His ways. For example, mammon says to buy and sell; God says to sow and reap. Mammon is anti-God.

When the Bible teaches about a spirit of anti-Christ being in the world, it is referring to the spirit of mammon. In the book of Revelation, the Antichrist will attempt to dominate people through the use of economics—preventing people from buying or selling unless they submit to him (Revelation 13:17). In this way, the brief rule of the Antichrist will be through the spirit of mammon.

Don't get the wrong idea. Money and mammon are not the same thing. Money is not inherently evil—it is neutral. It can be used for bad or for good. It can be submitted to God or to the spirit of mammon. One of the most frequently misquoted verses in the Bible is 1 Timothy 6:10: "For the love of money is the root of all evil." Of course, most people misquote this verse as "Money is the root of all evil." The Bible warns us that the love of (or worship of) money is the root of all kinds of evil. The idolatrous love of the spirit of mammon (or anti-Christ) is evil. When we serve mammon, we are allowing greed, covetousness, and selfishness, which are all manifestations of the spirit of mammon, into our lives.

The key to breaking a spirit of mammon is by tithing to your local church. Just as we discussed earlier in this series, when you tithe the first ten percent of your money, God redeems the other ninety percent. The ninety percent is submitted to God.

Money that is submitted to God and His purposes has God's Spirit on it, which is why it both multiplies and can't be consumed by the devourer. Money that has been submitted to God, or wealth devoted to serving Him rather than trying to replace Him, is blessed by God. In reality, God's Spirit blesses it. On the other hand, money that is not submitted to God has the spirit of mammon on it by default. That is why people often think money can bring them happiness or peace.

We can use money for unrighteous, temporal purposes, or we can use it for righteous, eternal purposes. The choice is ours. Consequently, we are to use money for what is eternal, such as bringing souls into God's kingdom. The reality is that all things in this world will be gone one day. God is going to make a new heaven and a new earth. The only things that will remain are souls.

In Luke 16, when Jesus tells us to use unrighteous mammon to gain friends, he is not telling us to simply gain friends here on this earth. He specifically says that we are to win friends for the day "when we fail," meaning when we die. Then, those friends we made will welcome us into our everlasting home. The only way your new friends can welcome you into an everlasting home is if they have been saved. Jesus is telling us to use money to bring people into the kingdom. The more people you bring into the kingdom, the more people there will be to welcome you into your eternal home.

Your money can be used to help people come to know Jesus. When you give your money to the local church, or to a ministry that helps people, your money is being used for God's purposes. If you were to give to a missionary and because of your gift, someone was saved, that person would be in heaven as a direct result of the way you used your money.

God says that those who are faithful with little will be entrusted with much. When we are faithful with the little things, like tithing and giving money to God's work, He will entrust us with true riches. True riches are people. Your money can be used to serve a spirit of mammon, or it can be used to build God's kingdom and bring more people into heaven.

TALK

For group discussion or personal reflection:

QUESTION 1

Have you ever been in a situation where you thought, "If I only had more money, I could fix this problem"? What did it feel like to be in this situation, and what was the result? If you are comfortable, tell about a time when this happened and how you responded.

_____

_____

_____

_____

QUESTION 2

Mammon deceives us by promising the things only God can give—security, significance, identity, independence, power, or freedom. In the past, which of these things have you been most likely to believe that wealth could give you?

_____

_____

_____

_____

QUESTION 3

Imagine a world where the love of money did not exist. What would the world look and feel like, and how would people behave? In your own words, describe how the world would look. Does it reflect anything you have read in the Bible? If so, explain.

_____

_____

_____

_____

_____

QUESTION 4

Jesus said that only those who are faithful in small things should expect to be entrusted with bigger things (Luke 16:10). What are some of the "small things" that God has entrusted to you? How can wise stewardship of those small things lead to bigger things?

_____

_____

_____

_____

_____

QUESTION 5

God is looking for good stewards to whom He can entrust more resources, because he knows they will faithfully invest in saving souls, help those who are hurting, and advance His kingdom. What are some key characteristics of a good steward?

_____

_____

_____

_____

_____

PRAY

Take some time as a group to pray for each other in the light of the truths discussed in this session.

EXPLORE

Do you want to go deeper with this teaching? Here are some additional things to think about, pray for, or write about in your journal throughout the next week:

KEY QUOTE

Heaven is being populated and hell is being plundered by our offerings.

—*Robert Morris*

What can you change about your current financial stewardship that would enable you to invest more in people?

_____

_____

_____

_____

Command those who are rich in this present age not to be haughty, nor to trust in uncertain riches but in the living God, who gives us richly all things to enjoy. Let them do good, that they be rich in good works, ready to give, willing to share, storing up for themselves a good foundation for the time to come, that they may lay hold on eternal life (1 Timothy 6:17-19).

I am:	Scripture References:
e.g., A beloved child of God	Galatians 3:26
	2 Corinthians 5:21
	Colossians 3:12
	Ephesians 1:6-8
	Romans 8:17

According to these verses, God wants to give us richly all we need to enjoy our lives as we trust Him and bless others. Write a few lines about what it is that you truly need to enjoy life. What makes life good?

_____

_____

_____

_____

_____

KEY VERSES

Luke 16:9-16, Romans 11:16, 1 Timothy 6:10

What stands out to you as you read these verses?

_____

_____

_____

_____

_____

What is the Holy Spirit saying to you through these Scriptures?

_____

_____

_____

_____

_____

KEY QUESTION

If you are not going to gain your identity from the quantity and variety of the things you own, then how does the Bible help you define your identity?

KEY PRAYER

Heavenly Father, I want everything in my life to be submitted to You—including my money. As I am obedient through tithing, I want Your Spirit to be on our money, not a spirit of mammon. Please guard my heart against the spirit of mammon that is so widespread in the world today. In Jesus' name, Amen.

05

AM I GENEROUS?

A very important question we all need to ask ourselves is "Am I generous?"
Selfishness is the enemy of generosity and tries to take the place of God.
A generous heart stems from a grateful heart.

RECAP

In the previous section, we explored the lies the spirit of mammon tells us about wealth. We learned that we could either submit our money to God or to a spirit of mammon. As you have worked through your finances this past week, in what ways have you been more aware of the battle between the spirit of mammon and the Spirit of God?

ENGAGE

Many great movies have been built around the theme of generosity versus selfishness: *It's a Wonderful Life, The Blind Side, A Christmas Carol, Pay it Forward, Schindler's List*, and *Casablanca* are just a few of those.

Choose one of these movies and discuss the ways generosity and selfishness are displayed in the film. Or choose another film in which generosity is a major theme and discuss its role in the film.

WATCH

Watch Robert Morris in "Am I Generous?" As you view it:

- Listen for the important word that only appears one time in the New Testament.
- Look for the reason why Mary would give such an extravagant gift.

(If you are not able to watch this teaching on video, read the following. Otherwise, skip to the **Talk** section after viewing.)

READ

Generosity and selfishness are at odds with one another. When faced with an opportunity to give, our hearts will gravitate either one way or the other. God is generous and Satan is selfish.

We are born selfish. In fact, one of the first words that a child learns to say well is "Mine!" And a child learns to say it at such a pitch that it will hit a nerve in the back of your neck. You'll be watching a sporting event or something else, and here's what you will hear from the other room: "Mine! Mine! Mine!" Normally this happens when a younger child pulls something away from an older child. The truth is we are all born selfish. The good news is that when we are born again, we are born generous. This doesn't mean Christians are always generous. But it does mean that instead of desiring to be selfish, we at least a desire to be generous. You still must crucify the "old man" and renew your mind so that you will grow in generosity the way God wants you to.

The Bible contains a great account that contrasts extravagant giving with a heart of selfishness:

> Then, six days before the Passover, Jesus came to Bethany, where Lazarus was who had been dead, whom He had raised from the dead. There they made Him a supper; and Martha served, but Lazarus was one of those who sat at the table with Him. Then Mary took a pound of very costly oil of spikenard, anointed the feet of Jesus, and wiped His feet with her hair. And the house was filled with the fragrance of the oil.
>
> But one of His disciples, Judas Iscariot, Simon's son, who would betray Him, said, "Why was this fragrant oil not sold for three hundred denarii and given to the poor?" This he said, not that he cared for the poor, but because he was a thief, and had the money box; and he used to take what was put in it.
>
> But Jesus said, "Let her alone; she has kept this for the day of My burial. For the poor you have with you always, but Me you do not have always" (John 12:1–8).

This amazing story demonstrates a sharp contrast between two kinds of hearts: The heart of Mary and the heart of Judas. The Gospel writer displays generosity and selfishness for us in one incident.

There's an incredible selfishness at work in Judas' heart in this account. He shows it in his comments about Mary's offering. Judas didn't actually care for the poor. He was a thief! Judas pretended that he was thinking about others while he was really only thinking of himself.

This same false spirituality shows up in similar comments we may hear today. "How could anyone in good conscience drive a car that expensive?" "She sure could have helped a lot of people for what she spent on that purse." Or, "I could do a lot of good with the money they spent on that [insert name of the item here]." Remarks such as these are invariably based on envy, jealousy, and selfishness dressed up as religious superiority—and it's the same spirit Judas had. As long as we can say, "Someone else isn't doing what they should be doing," and we don't even really know what they're doing, then we don't have to look inside of ourselves to see if we're generous or if we're selfish.

Jesus knew Judas was a thief, but He allowed Jesus to be in charge of the moneybox. Isn't that interesting? Jesus could have chosen any of His disciples to do that task. Then why did He choose Judas? Jesus didn't do this so Judas would fail; He did it so Judas would have an opportunity to pass the test. God will never tempt us, but He will test us. He will test us so we have the opportunity to succeed. God will actually test you in your finances and give you an opportunity to be successful.

Generosity is extravagant. God is an extravagant giver—He gave Jesus His Son for us. That kind of extravagance is difficult for our human minds to understand. There are examples of many other extravagant gifts in the Bible. David gave God the equivalent of

21 billion dollars. The widow who gave her two mites was an extravagant giver. She gave all she had. It is not the size of the money that counts, but the size of the heart in the offering.

When Mary gave the gift to Jesus in John 12, it was extravagant. Three hundred denarii was a very large sum of money. It was roughly equivalent to an entire year's wages. Of course, what constitutes a lot of money is relative depending on each person. What seems like a lot to the average person may not seem like much to a multimillionaire. But a year's income is a year's income, regardless of your income.

To understand the magnitude of this gift, think about your annual household income and imagine spending that amount on some perfumed oil. Now, imagine taking it and pouring it onto someone's feet. You are never going to get it back. It's been poured out. It's gone. However, it always makes sense to be generous toward God because He is always generous toward us. Actually, He is more than generous in His love toward us—He is extravagant.

How can we give an extravagant gift to God when He owns everything. Even boxes of gold would only be heavenly asphalt to Him. The gift of giving ourselves, our hearts, and our lives to God can be extravagant. It's the attitude. It's that you've given your heart to Him. And you can't say you've given God your heart if you haven't given Him your money—Scripture is clear that where your treasure is, there your heart will be also. So when God gets your heart, the fruit of that is visibly shown as you give to Him.

There are actually three levels of giving: tithes, offerings, and extravagant offerings. Some people joke that extravagant offerings are *painful* offerings. Only five to seven percent of Christians usually even get to the first level—that is shocking! The great news is that if you can get past the first level and tithe, the curse is broken and God generously blesses you, and it becomes easier to give offerings and even extravagant offerings.

When Mary poured the costly oil on Jesus' feet, it was an extravagantly generous offering. Why did she do this? Why did she give such and extravagant, generous gift to the Lord? Mary had a generous heart. She was grateful for all that Jesus had done for her. Just two months earlier, Jesus had raised her brother Lazarus from the dead. If one of your family members were raised from the dead, would you be grateful? All who believe in Jesus have been raised from the dead because we were all dead in our trespasses and sins. If you or anyone in your family has been born again, then all of you have been raised from the dead and have eternal life with Jesus in heaven. That is something to be grateful for!

Mary came to Jesus with a heart overflowing with gratitude and love. That love translated itself into worship through an offering that cost a great deal. In a similar way, we show God each week how much gratitude and love are in our hearts. So ask yourself this revealing question: "What do my offerings say about my level of gratitude and love for God?" We all battle selfishness. Generosity must always overcome selfishness in us. Real generosity is extravagant.

NOTES

_____

_____

_____

_____

_____

TALK

For group discussion or personal reflection:

QUESTION 1

As any parent can testify, children are born knowing how to be selfish. Selfishness comes naturally, but generosity must be learned and cultivated. Describe one of your earliest memories of wrestling with your own selfish nature.

_____

_____

_____

_____

_____

QUESTION 2

We usually find it easier to be generous in some areas of our lives rather that others (e.g., time, money, possessions, credit for accomplishments, etc.). In what areas of life have you found it easiest to be generous? In what areas have you found it most difficult?

_____

_____

_____

_____

_____

QUESTION 3

When the Holy Spirit prompts you to give an extravagant gift to the Lord or to His work, what kinds of emotions and thoughts rush in to discourage you from obeying?

_____

_____

_____

_____

_____

QUESTION 4

Robert Morris said the most extravagant gift we can give to God is ourselves. Do you agree or disagree? What does this look like for you personally in your daily life?

_____

_____

_____

_____

QUESTION 5

Describe an extravagant gift that you have given to another person or received from someone. What made it extravagant? What was the impact?

_____

_____

_____

_____

PRAY

Take some time as a group to pray for each other in the light of the truths discussed in this session.

EXPLORE

Do you want to go deeper with this teaching? Here are some additional things to think about, pray for, or write about in your journal throughout the next week:

KEY QUOTE

Generosity is when you give expecting nothing in return. Selfishness is when you give and think that God owes you something.

—Robert Morris

Take a moment to think about a talent, gift, or ability that you have. Now consider how you might be able to give your time in this area to bless a person, a ministry, or the church in an extravagant way. For example, if you are a doctor, how could you give of your services in an extravagant way? If you are an accountant, how could you give of your talent and time in an extravagant way to bless a life? Perhaps helping a single mom or a widow with their taxes would be an extravagant way of giving. If you are a stay-at-home mom, perhaps for you extravagant giving would be playing and engaging with your kids in extra special ways. The ideas can be as simple or complex as you want. Ask the Holy Spirit to direct you in the way God wants you to be an extravagant giver.

_____

_____

_____

_____

KEY VERSES

John 12:1-8, Proverbs 11:25, 2 Corinthians 8:3-5

What stands out to you as you read these verses?

_____

_____

_____

_____

What is the Holy Spirit saying to you through these Scriptures?

_____

_____

_____

_____

KEY QUESTION

In the Bible passages we read in this section, Mary gave Jesus a gift that cost about one year's wages. How much would that be for you if you gave Jesus a gift of that cost today?

The Bible records Mary's gift, which has been taught about for centuries and will be remembered for eternity. If eternity remembered an extravagant gift you gave to Jesus, what would you want it to be?

Take time this week to pray and ask God to show you the extravagant gift you can give to Him.

_____

_____

_____

_____

_____

KEY PRAYER

Heavenly Father, thank You for the extravagant gift of everlasting life that You have given us through Jesus Christ. We recognize Your great love for us. Help us not to hold anything back from You. Help us to give of our lives and resources for Your kingdom. We pray that we would never hold back out of fear, but we would always be able to trust that You are our promoter, protector, and provider. Thank You for Your great love. In Jesus' name, Amen.

06

THE PRINCIPLES OF MULTIPLICATION

The miracle of multiplication is available to God's people. But our resources must be "blessed" by Jesus. Then we must give those resources away before they can multiply.

RECAP

In the previous section, we explored the power of extravagant giving springing from a heart of generosity. How did this message challenge you as you thought about it this past week?

ENGAGE

You're going to host a big meal for a large group of friends or family. What's on the menu?

WATCH

Watch Robert Morris in "The Principles of Multiplication." As you view it:

- Look for the two keys to multiplication.

- Listen for three things Robert and Debbie Morris did to get their "financial house" in order.

(If you are not able to watch this teaching on video, read the following. Otherwise, skip to the **Talk** section after viewing.)

READ

Multiplication is a mathematical term like addition, subtraction, or division. But multiplication is better than addition when it comes to our resources. And our God is a God of multiplication. He is a God who can multiply. Would it be acceptable if God multiplied your resources?

The Gospel of Luke includes the account of one of those miraculous multiplications—the feeding of the 5,000 families. Luke tells us that there were 5,000 men. Additionally, there were women and children. Because of this, most Bible scholars estimate the crowd was easily more than 20,000 people.

When the day began to wear away, the twelve came and said to Him, "Send the multitude away, that they may go into the surrounding towns and country, and lodge and get provisions; for we are in a deserted place here." But He said to them, "You give them something to eat."

And they said, "We have no more than five loaves and two fish, unless we go and buy food for all these people." For there were about five thousand men.

Then He said to His disciples, "Make them sit down in groups of fifty." And they did so, and made them all sit down.

Then He took the five loaves and the two fish, and looking up to heaven, He blessed and broke them, and gave them to the disciples to set before the multitude. So they all ate and were filled, and twelve baskets of the leftover fragments were taken up by them (Luke 9:12-17).

Jesus first blessed the food, and then He gave it to the disciples to hand out to the crowd. The *first principle* of multiplication is that our resources must first be blessed by Jesus before they multiply. When we give the first of our increase—the tithe—to the Lord, the rest of it is blessed.

Many believers have never seen their finances multiply. Often, the reason is that their money hasn't been blessed. When you give it to the Lord first and the Lord puts His blessing on it, then—and only then—does it have the ability to multiply. Jesus—the One who receives our tithes—is the only One who has the power to bless our money so it can multiply.

The *second principle* is this: Only what is given away can multiply. In the example of the miraculous feeding in the Galilean countryside, the disciples held the bread and the fish. It had been blessed, so it had the potential to multiply. But if they had just eaten it themselves, it would have remained five loaves and two fish. It would never have multiplied—even though Jesus Himself had blessed it! Each of the disciples would have taken a couple of bites of food instead of everyone having full stomachs and twelve baskets of leftovers.

In the same way the disciples had to give away what they had for it to be multiplied, we have to give away what we have for it to multiply. This is another reason many believers never see the miracle of multiplication in their finances. Sometimes those who are tithing give little or nothing over and above the tithe. They don't realize that only that which is given away can multiply.

There is a difference between tithing and giving. Tithing is simply returning to God that which He said is His. Giving our firstfruits—our first ten percent to the Lord through a local church—is what causes that which is ours to be blessed.

You can't "give" something that doesn't really belong to you. The firstfruits belong to the Lord. The rest is yours to keep or give as you choose. It is from this account that you give what the Bible often refers to as offerings. Tithing isn't really giving—it's returning. It is bringing back to the Lord what is already His. Thus, the second principle of multiplication is that finances must be shared if they are to multiply.

Often God wants to bless our finances, but they are out of order. God cannot bless things that are out of order. When God spoke to Robert and Debbie Morris about getting their finances in order, this included getting out of debt, not manipulating, and giving.

In order for them to get out of debt, they had to sell a car they were driving that included a payment they couldn't afford. They bought another car for $750 and drove it in order to live below their means. It took them several years, but they were able to pay off all their debt.

When Robert was a full-time traveling evangelist, God spoke to him about not manipulating his finances. Whenever a church asked what his expenses were for coming to preach, God told him to tell the churches: "I have no financial requirements for coming." During this time, God taught Robert and Debbie to rely completely on the Lord for all their provision. They were diligent tithers, but God was about to teach them something new about giving and being generous.

During this season of their life, Robert and Debbie's entire income came from the love offerings that he received from the churches where he preached. One particular month, he was only scheduled to preach at one church. Thankfully, the love offering that evening was enough to cover their entire month's expenses. Earlier in that evening's worship service, a missionary had given a brief testimony and an update for the congregation. As he looked across the nearly empty sanctuary, Robert caught a glimpse of the missionary. As he did, the unmistakable voice of the Lord spoke in his heart: "I want you to give him your offering—all of it."

In obedience, Robert signed the check he had just received over to the missionary and asked the missionary not to say anything. Later that evening, they were eating pizza with some people from the church and a man asked to see the check he had just received. Robert responded that perhaps it was in the car, but the man insisted. The man then looked at him in the eyes and said, "I know you don't have the check. The Lord told me." Then the man handed Robert a check he had written before he came that was exactly ten times the amount of the first check. He said to Robert, "God is about to teach you about giving so that you can teach the Body of Christ."

A few years later, Robert was reading his Bible in the book of Philippians where Paul says Jesus gave up everything. Robert felt God speak to him: "Would you give Me everything?" So Robert and

Debbie emptied out all their savings accounts, checking accounts, and retirement accounts. They gave away their two cars. And they gave away their house. They gave away every asset they owned.

God did pour out His blessing on them after they gave extravagantly. However, the greatest blessing came when Robert was reading about Solomon a few weeks later. After Solomon gave an extravagant offering to the Lord (1,000 bulls rather than the tradition of 1 bull), God told Solomon, "Ask anything you want." Robert felt God tell him that same thing after his extravagant offering of giving all he owned. Robert's request was to stay passionately in love with Debbie for the rest of their lives. At the time of the message in this video, they have been married for 35 years! That is a gift from God!

TALK

For group discussion or personal reflection:

QUESTION 1

Read Hebrews 7:8. Only that which has been "blessed" by the Lord can multiply. The disciples put the loaves and fish into Jesus' hands so He could bless those things. How can we put the money that comes to us into Jesus' hands so He can bless it?

_____

_____

_____

_____

QUESTION 2

Why do you think Jesus instructed the disciples to divide the huge crowd into groups of 50? What areas of your life might require some organization and order before God can bring increase to them?

_____

_____

_____

_____

QUESTION 3

Tithing is bringing to God that which is rightfully His. It is when we give over and above the tithe that the miracle of multiplication takes place. How do you decide when, where, and how much to give?

_____

_____

_____

_____

_____

QUESTION 4

Describe a time when you have seen the principle of multiplication at work in your life or in someone else's life.

_____

_____

_____

_____

QUESTION 5

Hearing the Lord instruct you to give something—a car, a specific sum of money, or some other possession—obviously requires the ability to hear God's voice. Do you currently hear His voice in that way? In what ways can we become more sensitive to prompting and instructions from the Lord?

_____

_____

_____

_____

PRAY

Take some time as a group to pray for each other in the light of the truths discussed in this session.

EXPLORE

Do you want to go deeper with this teaching? Here are some additional things to think about, pray for, or write about in your journal throughout the next week:

KEY QUOTE

The Lord spoke to me one day in my quiet time, and He said, "I want you to get your finances in order so I can bless them."

—*Robert Morris*

GETTING YOUR FINANCES IN ORDER

Rank yourself on a scale of 1-10 (1 being the "worst" and 10 being "best") in the following areas:

Area:	Score:
Getting (and staying) out of debt	
Living within your means	
Having a budget/tracking expenses	
Praying about significant purchases	
Being accountable in your spending (e.g., to your spouse)	
Being diligent and faithful at work	

For you to get your finances in order, what areas need the most attention? Develop a plan to get your finances in order.

For help, visit: http://gatewaypeople.com/ministries/stewardship

_____

_____

_____

_____

KEY VERSES

Proverbs 22:9, John 12:24, Romans 11:16, 2 Corinthians 9:5-11, Luke 16: 9-13

What stands out to you as you read these Scriptures?

_____

_____

_____

_____

What is the Holy Spirit saying to you through these Scriptures?

_____

_____

_____

_____

KEY QUESTION

Are your finances blessed? And do you trust God enough to obey when He says to give, even when it doesn't seem there will be enough for other things? Why or why not?

_____

_____

_____

_____

KEY PRAYER

Father, make me "blessable!" Please build in me a grateful, audacious, courageous, and generous heart to give; for I know that this is the only way to experience true fulfillment, purpose, joy, and peace. I know that this is the key to living the blessed life. In Jesus' name, Amen.

NOTES

_____

_____

_____

_____

_____

_____

_____

_____

_____

_____

_____

_____

_____

_____

_____

LEADER'S GUIDE

The Blessed Life Leader's Guide is designed to help you lead your small group or class through *The Blessed Life* curriculum. Use this guide along with the curriculum for a life-changing, interactive experience.

BEFORE YOU MEET

- Ask God to prepare the hearts and minds of the people in your group. Ask Him to show you how to encourage each person to integrate the principles all of you discover into your daily lives through group discussion and writing in your journals.
- Preview the video segment for the week.
- Plan how much time you'll give to each portion of your meeting (see the suggested schedule below). In case you're unable to get through all of the activities in the time you have planned, here is a list of the most important questions (from the **Talk** section) for each week.

SESSION ONE

Q: Why do you think people sometimes struggle with selfishness before giving and grief after giving?

(Follow-up Question)

Can you think of a time you've struggled with either selfishness or grief when giving?

(Follow-up Question)

What are some practical ways you can work through those initial struggles in your heart and choose generosity with a grateful heart?

Q: People can give of their treasure, time, and talents. How does the way people spend their time, give of their treasure, and use their talents show the condition of their heart? In which of these areas are you the most generous?

SESSION TWO

Q: Many believers struggle when it comes to tithing. Why do you think this is? What are some of the barriers or misunderstandings that hinder believers from tithing?

Q: Hebrews 7:8 says that when we tithe here on earth, Jesus spiritually receives those tithes in heaven. How does that knowledge influence the attitude of your heart as you bring your tithes and offerings?

SESSION THREE

Q: What are some of the attributes of God that make you feel the most reverent or in awe of who He is? Does it make it easier or harder for you to honor God with your firstfruits when you take time to think about His attributes?

Q: Every time we are paid, an inescapable moment of "worship" immediately follows. The first place to which we direct a portion of that money reveals something about what is "first" in our lives. What kinds of financial things are most likely to compete for "first place" in our hearts?

SESSION FOUR

Q: Mammon lies to us by promising those things that only God can give, such as security, significance, identity, independence, power, or freedom. In the past, which of these have you been most likely to believe that wealth could deliver?

Q: Luke 16:10 says that only those who are faithful in small things should expect to be entrusted with bigger things. What are some of the "small things" with which we've been entrusted? And how can wise stewardship of those small things lead to bigger things?

SESSION FIVE

Q: We tend to find it easier to be generous in some areas of our lives than in others (e.g., time, money, possessions, credit for accomplishments, etc.). In what areas of life do you find it easiest to be generous. In what areas have you found it most difficult?

Q: When the Holy Spirit prompts you to give an extravagant gift to the Lord or to His work, what kinds of emotions or thoughts tend to rush in to discourage you from obeying?

SESSION SIX

Q: Why do you think Jesus instructed the disciples to divide the huge crowd into groups of 50? What areas of your life might require some organization and order before God can bring increase to them?

Q: Hearing the Lord instruct you to give something—a car, a specific sum of money, or some other possession—obviously requires the ability to hear God's voice. Do you currently hear His voice in that way? In what ways can we become more sensitive to prompting and instructions from the Lord?

Remember, the goal is not necessarily to get through all of the questions. The highest priority is for the group to learn and engage in a dynamic discussion.

HOW TO USE THE CURRICULUM

This study has a simple design.

EACH WEEK
THE ONE THING

This is a single statement under each session title that sums up the main point—the key idea—of the session.

RECAP

Recap the previous week's session, inviting members to share about any opportunities they have encountered throughout the week that apply what they learned (this doesn't apply to the first week).

ENGAGE

Ask the icebreaker question to help get people talking and feeling comfortable with one another.

WATCH

Watch the videos (recommended).

READ

If you're unable to watch the videos, read these sections.

TALK

Discuss the questions.

PRAY

Pray together.

EXPLORE

Encourage members to complete the written portion in their books before the next meeting.

KEY TIPS FOR THE LEADER

- Generate participation and discussion.
- Resist the urge to teach. The goal is for great conversation that leads to discovery.
- Ask open-ended questions—questions that can't be answered with "yes" or "no" (e.g., "What do you think about that?" rather than "Do you agree?").
- When a question arises, ask the group for their input instead of answering it yourself before allowing anyone else to respond.
- Be comfortable with silence. If you ask a question and no one responds, rephrase the question and wait for a response. Your primary role is to create an environment where people feel comfortable to be themselves and participate, not to provide the answers to all of their questions.
- Ask the group to pray for each other from week to week, especially about key issues that arise during your group time. This is how you begin to build authentic community and encourage spiritual growth within the group.

SUGGESTED SCHEDULE FOR THE GROUP

1. **Engage** and **Recap** (5 Minutes)
2. **Watch** and **Read** (20 Minutes)
3. **Talk** (30 Minutes)
4. **Pray** (10 minutes)

KEYS TO A DYNAMIC SMALL GROUP

RELATIONSHIPS

Meaningful, encouraging relationships are the foundation of a dynamic small group. Teaching, discussion, worship, and prayer are important elements of a group meeting, but the depth of each element is often dependent upon the depth of the relationships between members.

AVAILABILITY

Building a sense of community within your group requires members to prioritize their relationships with one another. This means being available to listen, care for one another, and meet each other's needs.

MUTUAL RESPECT

Mutual respect is shown when members value each other's opinions (even when they disagree) and are careful never to put down or embarrass others in the group (including their spouses, who may or may not be present).

OPENNESS

A healthy small group environment encourages sincerity and transparency. Members treat each other with grace in areas of weakness, allowing each other room to grow.

CONFIDENTIALITY

To develop authenticity and a sense of safety within the group, each member must be able to trust that things discussed within the group will not be shared outside the group.

SHARED RESPONSIBILITY

Group members will share the responsibility of group meetings by using their God-given abilities to serve at each gathering. Some may greet, some may host, some may teach, etc. Ideally, each person should be available to care for others as needed.

SENSITIVITY

Dynamic small groups are born when the leader consistently seeks and is responsive to the guidance of the Holy Spirit, following His leading throughout the meeting as opposed to sticking to the "agenda." This guidance is especially important during the discussion and ministry time.

FUN!

Dynamic small groups take the time to have fun! Create an atmosphere for fun, and be willing to laugh at yourself every now and then!